Language Classroom Assessment

Liying Cheng

English
Language
Teacher
Development
Series

Thomas S. C. Farrell,
Series Editor

Typeset in Janson and Frutiger
by Capitol Communications, LLC, Crofton, Maryland USA
and printed by Gasch Printing, LLC, Odenton, Maryland USA

TESOL International Association
1925 Ballenger Avenue
Alexandria, Virginia 22314 USA
Tel 703-836-0774 • Fax 703-836-7864

Publishing Manager: Carol Edwards
Cover Design: Tomiko Breland
Copyeditor: Jean House

TESOL Book Publications Committee
John I. Liontas, Chair

Maureen S. Andrade	Joe McVeigh
Jennifer Lebedev	Gail Schafers
Robyn L. Brinks Lockwood	Lynn Zimmerman

Project overview: John I. Liontas and Robyn L. Brinks Lockwood
Reviewer: Aubrey Bronson

ISBN 9781942223146

Contents

About the Author

Liying Cheng, PhD, is Professor in Language Assessment and Evaluation at the Faculty of Education, Queen's University, in Ontario, Canada. Her research interests include the impact of large-scale testing on instruction, relationships between assessment and instruction, and academic and professional acculturation of international and new immigrant students, workers, and professionals. She can be reached at liying.cheng@queensu.ca

Series Editor's Preface

The English Language Teacher Development (ELTD) Series consists of a set of short resource books for English language teachers that are written in a jargon-free and accessible manner for all types of teachers of English (native and nonnative speakers of English, experienced and novice teachers). The ELTD Series is designed to offer teachers a theory-to-practice approach to English language teaching, and each book offers a wide variety of practical teaching approaches and methods for the topic at hand. Each book also offers opportunities for teachers to interact with the materials presented. The books can be used in preservice settings or in-service courses and can also be used by individuals looking for ways to refresh their practice.

Liying Cheng's book *Language Classroom Assessment* explores different approaches to language assessment in the English language classroom. Cheng provides a comprehensive overview of different forms of language classroom assessment in an easy-to-follow guide that language teachers will find very practical for their own contexts. Topics covered include differences between testing and assessment, an overview of research associated with language classroom assessment, practices and tools, procedures, events and understandings, and giving feedback as well as assessment and motivation. *Language Classroom Assessment* is a valuable addition to the literature in our profession.

I am very grateful to the authors who contributed to the ELTD Series for sharing their knowledge and expertise with other TESOL professionals because they have done so willingly and without any compensation to make these short books affordable to language teachers throughout the world. It was truly an honor for me to work with each of these authors as they selflessly gave up their valuable time for the advancement of TESOL.

Thomas S. C. Farrell

Introduction to Language Classroom Assessment

After reading this chapter, you should be able to answer the following questions.

- What is language classroom assessment?
- What are the four major aspects of language classroom assessment?
- What research evidence do you need to know about language assessment?

Definition

Language testing and assessment is a relatively new field within the broad context of applied linguistics. This field is rooted in applied linguistics because language testing and assessment primarily deal with English language learners (ELLs) and test-takers, and consists of test designers, publishers, teachers, and researchers who have a strong interest in and influence on the teaching and learning of English around the world. The field also includes testing of languages other than English (e.g., the testing of Chinese as a second or foreign language). The major theoretical framework that guides the field of language testing and assessment is derived from educational measurement based on classical and modern test theory (e.g., Bachman, 1990) and theories from applied linguistics (e.g., Canale & Swain, 1980).

The nature of the field, as explained here, has reached two important landmarks: (1) what is at stake and important to the field (in this case, learners' learning of the English language and test-takers' test performance of the English language) and (2) the shift from a focus on testing to a focus on assessment. This shift synchronizes with the worldwide movement in general education to combine assessment *of* learning and assessment *for* learning. *Assessment of learning* refers to those assessments that happen after learning has occurred to determine whether learning has happened. They are used to make statements of student learning status at a point in time. *Assessment for learning* refers to the process of seeking and interpreting evidence for use by students and their teachers to decide where the students are in their learning, where they need to go, and how best to get there.

The terms *testing* and *assessment* are both used in this book to show the historical development of the field. First, the focus was on testing, and then the focus moved to assessment, which includes testing. This second, broad definition includes large-scale testing such as the Test of English as a Foreign Language (TOEFL) and the International English Language Testing System (IELTS) and the classroom tests and assessments that teachers design and use in their own classrooms. This book focuses on the classroom tests, assessments, theories, and practices that guide language classroom assessment.

The definition of assessment can include events, tools, processes, and decisions (Taylor & Nolen, 2008). These four aspects, which are also fundamental to language classroom assessment, are discussed in subsequent chapters:

- *Assessment events* can support students when the events occur with enough frequency that the teacher knows whether instruction is successful and which student or group of students may need additional support.

- *Assessment tools* can support student learning when the tools give students clear ideas about what is important to learn and the criteria or expectations for good work, and when assessment matches with instruction.

- *Assessment processes* can support students, in that students see teachers as allies to their education; feedback can help students focus and better understand requirements.

- *Assessment decisions* can support students when grades accurately reflect what students learn.

Testing and Assessment Experience

Teachers make decisions about assessment practices on a day-to-day basis. Their decisions are influenced to a large extent by individual past testing and assessment experiences. For example, research has demonstrated that learning from past experience changed the circuitry in individuals' brains; thus individuals can categorize what they have observed, make a decision, and carry out appropriate actions. When something positive results from a decision, individuals are more prone to decide in a similar way, given a similar situation. On the other hand, individuals tend to avoid repeating past mistakes. Therefore, it is important for teachers to pause and reflect on their own past testing and assessment to guide their current and future assessment practices. The following activity is designed to guide you in this reflection.

Activity

1. Reflect on one experience in your life that made you feel good about being assessed or taking a test. Alternatively, you may reflect on one experience in your life that made you feel terrible as a result of being assessed or taking a test.

   - What was the experience?

   - Which aspects of testing and assessment were related to that experience?

   - Was the experience related to test content, test tasks, test types, or how the test was administered or marked?

2. Write down the factors that you feel have contributed to your positive experience in taking a language test, for example,

   - clear test directions,

   - familiar test formats, and

   - other factors.

   and the factors that you feel that have contributed to your negative experiences, for example,

   - noisy testing environment,

   - too little time, and

   - other factors.

3. How do these positive or negative factors contribute to the validity and reliability of assessment?

Validity refers to the accuracy and appropriateness of the test score and use. *Reliability* refers to the consistency of the testing process in relation to test administration and scoring.

4. In Excerpts 1 and 2 below, read the test-takers' test-taking experiences. How do these experiences enhance or decrease the validity and reliability of assessment?

Excerpt 1. Negative Test-Taking Experience
(Cheng & Deluca, 2011, p. 110)

> I couldn't hear the tape clearly so I immediately told the invigilator and was sent to the special room (an alternate listening room). Already anxious about missing some listening materials, I was assigned to sit at the back of the room in front of windows that faced a basketball court. The door to my right was open, and I could hear the noise of students playing downstairs and of those walking past. A portable stereo player was placed on a chair at the front of the room. The volume was really low and I found it extremely difficult to follow the content.

Excerpt 2. Positive Test-Taking Experience
(Cheng & Deluca, 2011, p. 111)

> Usually when taking listening tests, the time limit is so tight it makes me nervous. Some tasks or questions appear after a long audio text such that test-takers have to memorize what they have just heard; the tests require test-takers to have good memory skills. In contrast, this listening test was chunked into four parts, and the first three parts were divided into further subparts. Before and after each part and subpart, sufficient time was given to test-takers to familiarize themselves with the questions or check their answers. These practices allow test-takers to feel at ease and enabled assessment of test-takers' listening ability—which should be the major criterion.

Excerpt 1 illustrates how test environmental factors contributed *negatively* to test-takers' perceptions of assessment fairness. Excerpt 2, on the other hand, describes a testing experience wherein time was managed so that this test-taker could effectively complete tasks and engage in deeper cognitive processes. Further, increasing timing and allowing breaks throughout the test was linked to reduced anxiety levels and better performance for this test-taker.

Understanding such testing and assessment experiences is essential for continued validation inquiry. Such inquiry can support teachers as they learn experientially and reflect critically on core aspects of assessment, such as construct representation (e.g., test administration and conditions, timing, test structure and content, and scoring) and construct-irrelevant variance (e.g., aspects of test use and consequences such as test coaching or preparation, emotions and self-efficacy, and misuses of test scores versus test purpose). Furthermore, understanding test-takers' experiences can illustrate the impact of test consequences on perceptions of test validity and help teachers to understand the interconnectedness of testing constructs, processes, and uses.

Language Testing and Assessment Research

Early developments in language testing and assessment were signified by the work of Oller (1979) on the nature of language ability as a single unitary construct (in which all four language skills are seen as a whole) and by the seminal work of Canale and Swain (1980) on the teaching and testing of language communicative competence. These works forced language testers to consider the sociolinguistic aspects of language use and the contexts in which language testing takes place. Canale and Swain's theoretical framework of communicative competence strongly influenced the working model of communicative language ability in language testing used by teachers and researchers. Bachman and Palmer (1996), language teachers in their early careers, pointed out that the working model of communicative language ability "provides a valuable framework for guiding the definition of constructs for any language testing development situation" (p. 67). Bachman (2000) further points out that language testing practice was informed "by a theoretical view of language ability as consisting of skills (listening, speaking, reading and writing) and components (e.g., grammar, vocabulary, pronunciation) and an approach to test design that focused on testing isolated 'discrete points' of language, while the primary concern was with psychometric validity and reliability" (pp. 2–3).

The current debate remains whether teachers should assess language skills and components separately or integrated in large-scale testing and in classroom assessment contexts. This debate has implications for teachers because teachers design and conduct their own classroom assessments. Following is an exploration of how language testing and assessment have developed as an interdisciplinary field of applied linguistics.

Three very important aspects in language testing and assessment represent the major developments in the field over the past 50 years: test validation, washback research, and emerging research into teachers' classroom assessment practices, including recent developments in diagnostic assessment. It is essential for teachers who are interested in refining the classroom practices they engage in on a day-to-day basis to understand all three aspects of development.

At the core of any testing inquiry is *validity*. Like teachers, test designers and test users want to be confident in the meaning that is attached to testing results and the consequences of those results. More specifically, establishing the validity of a test corresponds to the accuracy and appropriateness associated with assessing student ability (Messick, 1989). Although some of these frameworks focus on establishing internal validity through an examination of psychometric processes within testing programs, which deals with the design, administration, and interpretation of tests (Bachman, 2000), others maintain a broader scope, considering contextual factors and social consequences of test validity (McNamara, 2007). Across these frameworks, there is a growing emphasis on collecting validity evidence from multiple stakeholders (e.g., teachers and students who use the tests) and using multiple research methods (e.g., instructional data from your own classroom).

Alderson and Wall (1993) proposed 15 hypotheses regarding the potential influence of language testing on various aspects of language teaching and learning. Cheng, Watanabe, and Curtis (2004) made the first systematic attempt to capture the essence of the washback phenomenon. *Washback* refers to the relationship between testing, teaching, and learning. Through their collection of washback studies from around the world, they responded to the question *What does washback look like?* within the teaching and learning context. Since then, many large-scale empirical studies have been conducted by language teachers and researchers, and these studies have demonstrated the influence of testing on major aspects of teaching and learning. The results of these studies (e.g., Cheng, 2005) point to the urgent need for teachers to understand the nature of testing, to refine their own classroom assessment without unquestioningly accepting or following large-scale testing. Several other consequences have also been researched, including the cognitive aspects of testing (i.e., the cognitive processing of test tasks and formats), the use of test-taking strategies, the interaction of motivation and anxiety with test-takers' test performance, and the social aspects of testing (e.g., test-takers' perceptions and potential test uses or misuses within a specific context; see Cheng, 2008).

Only recently have studies of the assessment practices used by teachers of English started to emerge (Rea-Dickins, 2004; Brindley, 2007). Studies of classroom assessment practices used by teachers of English have been relatively limited compared with the fairly large body of studies of large-scale language testing practices in the field. What has been done so far has shown that teachers' assessment practices are often influenced by external testing, and these studies further identified a lack of assessment training in teacher education (Cheng, 2005). Breen et al. (1997) and Cumming (2001) found clear links between the instructional and assessment purposes held by English language teachers and the assessment practices they used.

Assessment *for* learning is currently one of the most talked about pedagogical approaches for enhancing student achievement. Teachers, as the agents of assessment, need to ensure the reliability and validity of their classroom assessment practices and use these practices in ways that support their students' learning (Black & Wiliam, 1998a, 1998b). Consequently, an increasing number of attempts have been made to adapt large-scale language testing to serve the purpose of supporting students' learning. However, the key to such classroom practice success in supporting student learning resides in *you*, as teachers, on using quality classroom assessment practices.

Based on the research evidence and developments discussed above, we know the field of language testing and assessment continues to work on assessment of language skills and components, to focus on the accuracy and appropriateness of test score interpretation, and, increasingly, to focus on the sociocultural context where testing and assessment take place. This concept of teaching and assessing language ability within context enables us to understand the interaction between the test, test-takers, and interlocutors (raters, markers, and teachers) within context. This concept also supports us in designing our own assessment, taking consideration of aspects of an assessment task. This particular focus has a great deal to offer in relation to how assessing the integrated skills should be conducted and marked as well as how and how fast feedback of test performance should be communicated to test-takers. This focus also has significance for language classroom assessment that teachers conduct on a day-to-day basis.

To emphasize, three aspects of research studies—test validation, washback research, and emerging research into teachers' classroom assessment practices (which is the focus of this book)—all have implications on how teachers design and conduct their day-to-day classroom assessment.

2

Language Classroom Assessment Practices

After reading this chapter, you should be able to answer the following questions:

- What are teachers' classroom assessment practices?
- What are the purposes of language classroom assessment?
- What are the methods of language classroom assessment?
- What are the procedures of language classroom assessment?

Language Classroom Assessment Practices

For the past 50 years, studies in the field of language testing have focused on large-scale testing (Bachman, 2000) and its impact on teaching and learning (Alderson & Wall, 1993; Cheng, 2005). Despite the large number of students who are learning English around the world, studies of the assessment practices used by their teachers of English are only emerging (e.g., Cheng, Rogers, & Hu, 2004; Cheng, Rogers, & Wang, 2008; Davison, 2007). Breen et al. (1997) and Cumming (2001) found clear links between the instructional and assessment purposes held by English language instructors and the assessment practices they used. Further, Rea-Dickins' (2004) and Brindley's (2007) studies consist of the major empirical research recently conducted in language testing with teachers of English in different parts of the world, including Australia, Great Britain, Canada, Europe, and China. These studies illustrate the essential role of assessment in English language teaching and learning, as well as the relationship between assessment and student learning. Cheng, Rogers, and Hu (2004) conducted one of the first studies on teachers' assessment practices (see also Cheng, Rogers, & Wang, 2008). These studies compared classroom assessment practices by English language teachers in three tertiary institutional contexts—Canada, Hong Kong, and China—and showed that teachers' preferences for different methods of assessment were influenced by beliefs they held about assessment, their assessment purposes, their teaching experiences and educational training, and the nature of their instructional contexts (such as the instructional goals of the program, class size, and the dominance of external large-scale high-stakes testing).

In addition, more studies have been conducted on school-based assessment (e.g., Davison, 2007), which has already seen an impact within the Hong Kong education system. As mentioned above, assessment *for* learning, including school-based assessment, is currently one of the most talked-about pedagogical approaches for enhancing student achievement. This concept has significant implications for both teaching and learning and presents challenges to definitions of key components of assessment such as validity, reliability, and fairness at the philosophical, theoretical, and practical levels.

Nature of Classroom Assessment Practices

Teachers' values and beliefs about teaching and learning, and their considerations of the purposes and consequences of assessment, provide a strong rationale for their assessment decision making. From a systematic review of 40 entries in the classroom assessment literature, Brookhart (2004) found that the practice of educational assessment occurred at the intersection of three practical bases—instruction, classroom management, and classroom assessment—and at the intersection of three theoretical bases—psychology, sociology, and measurement. She recommended that in order to evaluate the meaning, value, accuracy, and consistency of classroom assessment information, the intersection and interdisciplinary nature of classroom assessment should be acknowledged in order to understand the complexity of teachers' classroom assessment practices. The practical bases of instruction, classroom management, and classroom assessment decide the kinds of practices that teachers undertake. There are no right or wrong practices, but teachers need to be acutely aware that their assessment

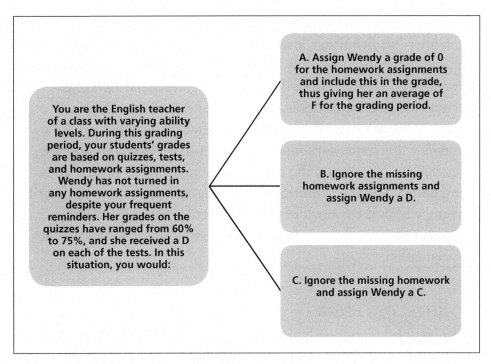

Figure 1. Interaction of Instruction, Classroom Management, and Classroom Assessment (Sun & Cheng, 2013)

practices are driven by their decisions. The scenario in Figure 1 best describes the complex situation that teachers deal with in their day-to-day assessment practices.

Research on classroom assessment practices revealed that the day-to-day assessment of student learning is unquestionably one of the teacher's most demanding, complex, and important tasks. Every model of the teaching and learning process requires that teachers base their decisions—instructional, grading, and reporting—on some knowledge of student progress toward desired learning outcomes (Taylor & Nolan, 2008). Teachers, as the agents of assessment, need to ensure the validity and reliability of their classroom assessment practices and use these practices in ways that support their students' learning (Black & Wiliam, 1998a, 1998b). The synergy of assessment *for* learning punctuated with the use of assessment *of* learning, strongly rooted in both educational measurement and language assessment, will best support student learning (Stiggins, 2005).

Black and Wiliam (1998b) define classroom assessment broadly to include all activities that teachers and students undertake to get information that can be used diagnostically to alter teaching and learning. Under this definition, assessment encompasses teacher observation, classroom discussion, and analysis of student work, including homework and tests. Within this framework, teachers' assessment practices include events, tools, processes, and decisions (Taylor & Nolan, 2008), as mentioned previously. Teachers need to learn how to *translate* this framework into their day-to-day classroom practices. They need to understand the major components of classroom assessment, understand the definition of learning and the models to describe learning within the context of their instruction, and explore their methods and procedures in relation to their purposes of assessment and evaluation.

REFLECTIVE BREAK

Following are some important questions on the interrelationship between teaching, learning, and assessment that will align what you teach and what you assess to support students' learning.

- What are my students supposed to learn (learning goals and objectives)?

- How do I teach so that my students learn? What do they do, and what do I do?

- How will I know whether my students have learned?

Classroom Assessment Events and Decisions

Taylor and Nolan's (2008) framework on assessment events, tools, processes, and decisions provides some of the best guidance for teachers' assessment practices. In this framework, *assessment events* can support students when the events occur with enough frequency that the teacher knows whether instruction is successful and which student or group of students may need additional support. *Assessment decisions* can support students when grades accurately reflect what students learn. Assessment events and decisions are discussed first here because they answer the question of the *why* of assessment. This is followed by a discussion of assessment *tools*—the *what* of assessment. The discussion of assessment *processes*—the *how* of assessment in relation to feedback and motivation—is discussed in Chapter 3. These four components are not sequential but are interrelated and happen simultaneously in teachers' instructional decisions and classroom practices.

Activity

Why do teachers assess their students? Look at the purposes of assessment in Table 1 and see if you can put them into the following three categories: student-centered purposes, instructional purposes, and administrative purposes. Some examples are given under each category below for illustration. Put your own purposes in the blanks. (To learn about how a group of 267 English language teachers categorized these purposes, see Cheng, Rogers, & Hu, 2004, pp. 367–368, for more information.)

Table 1. Purposes of Assessment and Evaluation

Purpose
To group my students for instruction purposes in my class
To obtain information on my students' progress
To plan my instruction
To diagnose strengths and weaknesses in my own teaching and instruction
To provide feedback to my students as they progress through the course
To motivate my students to learn
To encourage my students to work harder
To prepare my students for standardized tests (e.g., the TOEFL) they will need to take in the future
To diagnose strengths and weaknesses in my students
To formally document growth in learning
To determine the final grades for my students
To provide information to the central administration (e.g., school, university)
To provide information to an outside funding agency

- Student-centered purposes
  - Obtain information on my students' progress
  - Provide feedback to my students
  - Determine final grades for my students
  - _____

- Instructional purposes
  - Plan my teaching
  - Diagnose strengths and weaknesses
  - _____

- Administrative purposes
  - Provide information to the central administration
  - _____

Understanding why assessment is conducted is the most important first step in teachers' assessment decisions. The purposes of assessment influence the frequency and timing of assessment (*events*), the assessment methods used (*tools*), and how assessment is conducted (*processes*). These assessment purposes listed in Table 1 are not exclusive, and they are not good or bad. They are simply the reality of classroom instruction. The key is for teachers to contemplate the impact of these purposes on how assessment practices might be conducted differently in relation to the assessment tools used and the assessment processes created. Only by making this conscious effort can teachers ensure a higher quality of classroom assessment practices.

Classroom Assessment Tools

Assessment tools can support student learning when they give students clear ideas about what is important to learn and the criteria or expectations for good work, and when assessment matches with instruction. While you explore the assessment tools you use, you can reflect on what methods best help your students to achieve their learning goals and how to use various assessment methods to support all students. A combined use of assessment tools of receptive and productive language skills, language components (e.g., grammar, vocabulary, pronunciation), and direct and indirect assessment of skills can help to enhance the validity and reliability of assessment practices.

Activity

1. List all of the different ways, methods, and tools that have been used to assess you as a student or that you have used to assess your own students, or list the ways, methods, and tools you are aware of but have not used before, for example,

   - Essay questions
   - Multiple-choice questions
   - True and false questions
   - Oral presentation
   - Portfolio
   - Self-assessment
   - _____

2. Now can you categorize them into the following groups?

   - Supply type of questions
     — Essay questions
     — Oral presentation

     — _____

   - Selected type of questions
     — Multiple-choice questions
     — True and false questions

     — _____

   - Student-centered assessment
     — Self-assessment
     — Portfolio

     — _____

A sample of student-centered assessment can be as simple and informal as the exercise in Figure 2.

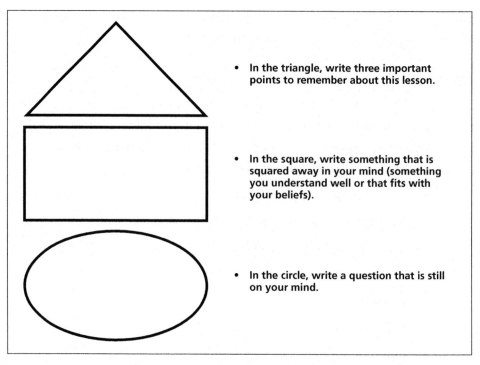

Figure 2. Triangle, Square, and Circle Summary (Tully, 2004)

You can explore more specific assessment tools in each of the skill areas: reading, writing, and speaking and listening. Then you can place these assessment tools into the following three categories and map each of the language skill areas onto your own classroom practices:

- teacher-made assessment methods
- student-conducted assessment methods
- standardized testing in reading, writing, and speaking and listening

These three categories are based on the research and represent major assessment constructs that guide teachers' assessment practices in the United States and Canada (see the Code for Fair Testing Practices for Education [http://www.apa.org/science/programs/testing/fair-testing .pdf], Principles for Fair Student Assessment Practices for Education in Canada [http://www2.education.ualberta.ca/educ/psych/crame/files /eng_prin.pdf], and Standards for Teacher Competence in Educational Assessment of Students [http://www.behavioralinstitute.org/Free

Downloads/Assessment/Teacher%20standards%20for%20assessment
.pdf]).

Teacher-made assessment methods refer to those designed and administered by teachers *to* their students, whereas *student-conducted* assessment methods refer to those that directly involve students' participation in the assessment process. It should be pointed out that other terms, such as *select*, *supply-type*, or *performance-based*, are also used to refer to the different assessment methods in the field of education. The three categories above best summarize the assessment approaches in an assessment *for* learning context, and can guide teachers in thinking about their own assessment practices. The more that assessment practices directly involve students, the more students feel a sense of their learning progress and the more they take responsibility for their own learning. Ultimately, only when students *want* to learn will they be able to learn. Assessment practices are there to support students' in learning.

REFLECTIVE BREAK

- What assessment methods do you use to evaluate your students?

- Which methods do you use the most? Which methods do you use the least?

The assessment methods in Tables 2–4 are commonly used to assess the students' learning of English (Cheng, Rogers, & Hu, 2004). First, contemplate the methods you actually use by putting a check mark (✓) for reading (Table 2), writing (Table 3), and speaking and listening (Table 4). If you use other methods not listed, write them down in the spaces provided because they are equally relevant to your assessment practice. Second, in the Rank column rank the methods you checked, starting with *1* for the method you use the most, *2* for the second most, *3* for the third most, and continue until you have ranked all the methods you checked off in the first column. Rank only the methods that you indicated you use. There is no right or wrong answer to your choices; rather, this two-phase activity helps you to reflect on

Table 2. Reading

Methods I use to assess reading (✓)	Assessment method	My ranking
	1. Read aloud or dictation	
	2. Oral interviews or questioning	
	3. Teacher-made tests containing	
	a. cloze items	
	b. sentence-completion items	
	c. true or false items	
	d. matching items	
	e. multiple-choice items	
	f. interpretative items (e.g., reading a passage or interpreting a map or a set of directions)	
	g. forms (e.g., an application form or an order form)	
	h. short-answer items	
	i. editing a piece of writing	
	4. Student summaries of what is read	
	5. Student journal	
	6. Student portfolio	
	7. Peer assessment	
	8. Self-assessment	
	9. Standardized reading tests	
	10. Other _____	
	11. Other_____	

your assessment practices. As a teacher, you use various assessment methods to achieve instructional, assessment, and classroom management goals. (See Cheng, Rogers, & Hu, 2004, and Cheng, Rogers, & Wang, 2008, for information about English language teachers in other contexts.)

Table 3. Writing

Methods I use to assess writing (✓)	Assessment method	My ranking
	1. Teacher-made tests containing	
	a. true or false items	
	b. matching items	
	c. multiple-choice items to identify grammatical error(s) in a sentence	
	d. editing a piece of writing such as a sentence or a paragraph	
	e. short essay	
	f. long essay	
	2. Student journal	
	3. Peer assessment	
	4. Self-assessment	
	5. Student portfolio	
	6. Standardized writing tests	
	7. Other: _____	
	8. Other: _____	

Now continue to reflect on the assessment tools you use in your own classroom by answering the following Reflective Break questions.

REFLECTIVE BREAK

Which assessment tools

- yield useful feedback to students?

- are most likely to be motivating to students?

- are easier to design and to score (feasibility of assessment)?

- provide the most *direct* information about a student's performance without interference by confounding factors?

Table 4. Speaking and Listening

Methods I use to assess oral skills (✓)	Assessment method	My ranking
	1. Oral reading or dictation	
	2. Oral interviews or dialogues	
	3. Oral discussion with each student	
	4. Oral presentations	
	5. Public speaking	
	6. Teacher-made tests asking students to	
	a. give oral directions	
	b. follow directions given orally	
	c. provide an oral description of an event or object	
	d. prepare summaries of what is heard	
	e. answer multiple-choice test items following a listening passage	
	f. take notes	
	g. retell a story after listening to a passage	
	7. Peer assessment	
	8. Self-assessment	
	9. Standardized speaking test	
	10. Standardized listening tests	
	11. Other: _____	
	12. Other: _____	

These questions may lead you to reexamine your decisions on assessment tools. The better you guide your assessment in these areas, the more likely you will achieve validity and reliability in your assessment practices. For example, you could try to use the assessment tools that provide your students with the most useful feedback or that best motivate your students. Remember, your students are going to be motivated in different ways based on their own learning characteristics. This will require you as a teacher to use various assessment tools. As part of the classroom reality, you will also need to consider the feasibility of your assessment practices. For example, designing multiple-choice items takes a long time but is an easier format to grade, whereas essay questions are relatively easy to design yet take a long time to mark and provide feedback. You will need to balance the use of these tools at different stages of your instruction. In the end, you will want to use as many direct assessment tools (e.g., oral presentations to assess students' oral ability) as you can. However, such assessment takes a long time and you will need to maintain sufficient instructional time. Again you will need to make some tough assessment choices in your own classroom.

Classroom Assessment Procedures

Your classroom assessment practices are part of your classroom instruction, and such practices are intertwined with the classroom reality. This section helps you to rethink your assessment practices in terms of the sources of your assessment tools, the tools you use to provide feedback and report to your students, and the percentage of time you spend on assessment in relation to your instructional activities. Note that sometimes instructional and assessment activities are the same.

Activity

Three aspects below are important for you to explore.

- What are the sources of your assessment items?
- What are the methods that you use to provide feedback and report to your students?
- How much time do you devote to assessment activities in relation to your teaching?

1. Check (✓) which of the following represents your primary sources for assessment items. Write down any other sources.
   - Items developed by myself _____
   - Items prepared by other teachers _____
   - Items from published textbooks _____
   - Items from mandated syllabuses or curricula _____
   - Items found on the Internet _____
   - Other published assessment or test items _____
   - Other (specify) _____ _____

2. When you give feedback to your students during instruction, how do you provide that feedback? Check (✓) all that apply.
   - Verbal feedback _____
   - Checklist _____
   - Written comments _____
   - Teaching diary or log _____
   - Conference with student _____
   - Total test score _____
   - A letter grade _____
   - Other (specify): _____ _____

3. When you give a final report to your students, how do you provide that information? Check (✓) all that apply.
   - Checklist _____
   - Written comments _____
   - Teaching diary or log _____
   - Conference with student _____
   - Total test score _____
   - A letter grade _____
   - Other (specify): _____ _____

4. Approximately what percentage of the total instruction and assessment time per term or semester do you spend preparing for an assessment, collecting the assessment information, scoring the responses, and reporting assessment results? Include time spent both at school and at home. Check (✓) one of the options.

5% ____   30% ____

10% ____   40% ____

15% ____   50% ____

20% ____   more than 50% ____

Taken together, teachers' assessment decisions, events, tools, and procedures demonstrate the complexity of assessment and evaluation practices in English language contexts. These complex practices are clearly demonstrated in each of the assessment purposes (student-centered, instruction-centered, and administration-related), methods (teacher-made, student-made, and standardized testing in reading, writing, and speaking and listening), and procedures (sources, method of feedback, reporting, and time spent) that you worked through in the previous Activity. The context of your teaching determines the kinds of practices you choose. Instruction and assessment are integral parts of one another and influence each other in the day-to-day decisions teachers make in classroom teaching. This endeavor involves complex decision making.

In reading this chapter, challenge yourself further to explore the questions in the following Reflective Break. These questions will help you to rethink the complex relationship between assessment purposes, methods, and procedures. These questions also will push you to revisit the fundamental aspects of assessment (e.g., the use and interpretation of assessment information, which aspects have the greatest impact on students).

Reflective Break

- Who are the primary users of the data or information from your assessment methods?
    - Teachers
    - Students
    - Parents
    - Schools, universities, or colleges
    - Funding agencies
    - Government

- Who in those categories makes decisions based on the information? Are they users, decision makers, or objects or subjects of the decision?

- What will happen when the subjects of these assessment decisions (i.e., your students) have no say or do not use any assessment tools? In your assessment practices, should you involve your students as much as possible?

3

The Role of Assessment in Supporting Teaching and Learning

After reading this chapter, you should be able to answer the following questions.

- What is the core issue of assessment processes?

- What is role of feedback in assessment? How can you provide quality feedback?

- What is the relationship between assessment and motivation?

- How can you use assessment to motivate student learning?

This chapter addresses some of the most challenging aspects in teaching: deciding what to teach, what to assess, and how to reinforce the assessment processes to support learning. Look at Figure 3 and explore what it means to you as a teacher in achieving the crucial alignment of instructional goals with your teaching and assessment. Teachers need to constantly ask themselves *Have my students learned? And how well have they progressed through assessment practices?* The assessment box illustrates the *why*, *what*, and *how* of your assessment.

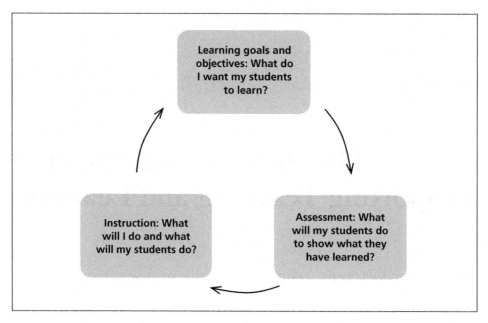

Figure 3. Relationship Between Learning Goals, Instruction, and Assessment (adapted from Taylor & Nolen, 2008, p. 41)

Activity

A quick way of assessing your students' learning by the end of each lesson is to do a 3-2-1 activity. If you do this as a speaking activity, you can divide the class into groups: One does the speaking, the other listens and takes notes. Have your students respond in writing or orally to the following:

- 3 new things I have learned
- 2 new ideas that occurred to me
- 1 important connection I made

Key to Assessment Processes: Feedback

Feedback is closely related to assessment processes. *Assessment processes* can support students in that students see teachers as allies to their education; feedback can help students focus and better understand the requirements.

If you have recently been in a student role yourself, reflect on some of the feedback you received from your teacher on your work. Describe your experience. In your description, include your answers to the following questions. If you have not been in this role lately, ask yourself how your students might have felt receiving your feedback.

- How did you feel when you received the feedback, and why?

- What did you learn from the feedback?

- What additional information would have been helpful?

Increasing expectations and accountability in education have resulted in the growing use of large-scale testing of school-aged students. This phenomenon has a tremendous impact on the continuing education of teachers in assessment literacy. This section focuses on one of the key aspects of assessment *for* learning: teachers providing feedback in assessment processes. The section will first unpack the nature of the feedback and then offer specific guidance on how teachers can provide constructive writing feedback. The section will then discuss the relationship of assessment and motivation to revisit the role feedback plays in assessment practices.

For assessment *for* learning to take place, the assessment processes need to involve the kinds of instructional activities that are likely to result in improving student performance. When it comes to teachers' decisions on assessment processes, the core link between the three questions in the Reflective Break above is the quality of *feedback*. The quality of teacher feedback (the way feedback is provided) signals to students that teachers are their allies and the teachers' role is to support student learning—not to rank students or compare students against each other. Rather, teacher feedback is meant to support students' growth over time in relation to the curriculum expectations and their own learning goals. The quality of teacher feedback (the detailed feedback provided) directs students' attention to areas of the curriculum in which they do well and in which they need further improvement so they understand the learning requirements better. Only by knowing where to go and what to do in their learning can students effectively improve their own performance. The quality of teacher feedback (and the timing of feedback as well) offers support for effective learning to take place. Feedback should

- be clear
- be encouraging
- be consistent with curriculum and assignment guidelines
- provide opportunities for improvement and continued learning
- be timely
- focus on key errors

The key errors in the English language are listed below, in order from most to least serious. You should provide feedback on no more than two areas each time to make sure that your feedback reaches your students and is integrated into their learning.

- verb forms (agreement, tense, etc.)
- word choice
- articles and prepositions
- spelling

Activity

Provide feedback to the essay in Figure 4 using the guidance provided above. Make sure that you provide feedback

- matching certain learning goals
- within a clearly defined timeline agreed upon with the student
- as to how this student can improve

According to Black and Wiliam (1998a), feedback is a critical characteristic of assessment *for* learning. Previous research studies have established that, although student learning can be advanced by feedback through comments, giving numerical scores or grades has a negative effect, and also students may ignore the comments given. You may have discovered this in your own teaching experience. A numerical score or grade does not tell students how to improve their work, so

> *I think it is better to be an only child. Firstly, you do not have to share your parents money. If I have older siblings, my parents will buy many things same my siblings, maybe I don not like it, but I can not change it. If I have younger siblings, when I bought one new thing, my siblings will want to have one thing better than mine. I think it is a big problem for my parents and me. Secondly, older siblings always have to take care of younger siblings. If I am a younger child in my family, maybe I will like have siblings, because I am a younger child, they should to take care about me, that is good. If I am an older child in my family, I should to be a rule model for my little brother or sister, and if they do something wrong, my parents will to criticize me, like I was not to take care of my siblings. That is really unfair. I do not like to take care of kids, they always cry, always want I play with them and want I buy something for them. If they let me to do these things, I will be crazy. Finally, I do not like other person look like me. If I have siblings, we have same parents, so we should look similar, and we can do similar things, I do not like a person really like me in this world. I know if I have siblings, we are all like want kill each other when we were young, I do not want this thing happen. I have many cousins, they are all like my siblings, so I do not need any siblings. Therefore, it is better to be an only child.*

Figure 4. Sample Student Writing

an opportunity to enhance their learning is lost. When giving students feedback, it is the nature, rather than the amount, of commentary that is critical.

Because feedback is a powerful way to affect student achievement, it is consistently ranked among the strongest interventions at a teacher's disposal (Fisher & Frey, 2009). Teachers need to know how to create feedback and also how to teach students to make use of the feedback they receive. According to Fisher and Frey (2009), feedback is a complex construct with three distinct components: feed up, feedback, and feed forward. To fully implement feedback, all these components must be used. In *feed up*, teachers must clearly articulate learning goals for their students. As a result, students will be more focused if they know their purposes for learning. In *feedback*, the teacher responds to students' work through descriptive feedback that is directly related to the learning goals. In doing so, the teacher provides an opportunity for the students to use the feedback to improve their work. Finally, *feed forward* enables the teacher to modify future instruction by using knowledge of students' progress.

REFLECTIVE BREAK

Now revisit the student writing sample in Figure 4 and provide feedback again according to the three components of *feed up, feedback*, and *feed forward.*

By implementing this feedback process into assessment *for* learning as a formative assessment tool, teachers are able to help students develop and acquire the knowledge and skills they need to learn. To be effective, feedback should encourage thinking to take place. Teachers can modify the specific framework of feed up, feedback, and feed forward offered by Fisher and Frey (2009) to meet their own students' learning needs. Overall, the implementation of this feedback system can and should change both teachers' and students' attitudes toward assessment practices. Instead of perceiving the assessment of their work as competitive and judgmental, students are able to use feedback as a distinct step in learning.

Assessment and Motivation

It is not surprising that assessment and motivation are closely related. What teachers assess and how they assess it influence most how students learn—how students see themselves as learners and how they see their learning reflect who they are as human beings. In day-to-day classroom practices, teachers' use both assessment *for* learning and assessment *of* learning. This combination requires teachers to do both *summative assessment* (involving the evaluation of learning with a mark or a score) and *formative assessment* (providing quality feedback). Both practices have tremendous impact on students, and both are necessary in classroom instruction. Three main aspects of assessment highlight the relationship of assessment and motivation:

1. Assessment and motivation require quality of feedback, that is, feedback needs to be

   - clear
   - focused
   - applicable
   - consistent
   - timely

2. Assessment and motivation address individual student needs, including

   - student differences
   - students' prior knowledge and experience
   - more use of self-assessment
   - more encouragement of self-directedness
   - more student reflections
   - more challenge to take responsibility in their own learning
   - more challenge to work toward their own learning goals

3. Assessment and motivation engage students by

   - making assessment real (i.e., contextual to students)
   - offering them choices in assessment tasks, tools, and procedures
   - helping them feel like they belong to the learning community
   - including them in assessment processes
   - creating a collaborative nature of assessment where students see teachers as allies

Two simple additional ideas are worth mentioning:

- The 5 *C*'s of assessment in general are *clarity*, *coherence*, *collaboration*, *communication*, and *care*.

- The 3 *F*'s in assessment are *feed up*, *feedback*, and *feed forward*.

Assessment, Learning, and Self-Determination Continuum

The role of assessment in motivating students to learn can be traced to many theories of motivation (Dörnyei, 2001). There are theories that focus on reasons for engagement in tasks; theories that focus on integrating expectancy and value constructs; and theories that integrate motivation and cognition. Particularly fitting for the assessment context is self-determination theory, introduced by Ryan and Deci (2000), who have further developed notions of intrinsic and extrinsic motivation, and on the relationship of these to the three basic human needs for autonomy, competence, and relatedness. Self-determination theory categorizes types of human motivation along a continuum from self-determined forms of intrinsic motivation to controlled forms of extrinsic motivation, and finally to amotivation, depending on degrees of self-determination. Testing and assessment policies are mostly based on the concept that rewards, punishments, and self-esteem–based pressures are effective motivators for learning. Self-determination theory thus fits well in the assessment context.

Ryan and Deci (2000) distinguished four types of motivation (from most self-determined to least self-determined): (a) intrinsic motivation, (b) self-determined extrinsic motivation, (c) non–self-determined extrinsic motivation, and (d) amotivation. *Intrinsic motivation* refers to motivation that makes one feel engaged in an activity that is inherently interesting or enjoyable. If the assessment practices teachers employ make students feel learning is interesting and enjoyable (make assessment real to students), then students will be intrinsically motivated.

In contrast, *extrinsically motivated* behaviors are instrumental in nature. Engaging in an activity with extrinsic motivation leads to a separable outcome. Self-determined extrinsic motivation is present when individuals participate in an activity voluntarily because the activity is valued and perceived to be of importance. It is extrinsic because the reason for participation is not within the activity itself but is a means to an end, and at the same time it is self-determined because the individual has decided and experienced a sense of direction and purpose in acting. If the assessment practices teachers employ make students feel that their learning is an important process for self-improvement, students may have self-determined extrinsic motivation to learn.

Non–self-determined extrinsic motivation occurs when individuals' behaviors are regulated by external factors such as rewards, constraints, or punishment. This type of motivation is extrinsic because the reason individuals participate in an activity lies outside the activity itself (e.g., family pressure); that is, the behavior is not self-determined. Individuals always experience an obligation to engage and are regulated by external rewards, constraints, or punishment. If the assessment practices teachers employ make students feel that their learning is driven by external rewards such as a bonus in grades or praise from teachers, students are non–self-determined extrinsically motivated.

Amotivation features the absence of intrinsic and extrinsic motivation. It is the state of lacking an intention to act. In this case, students feel that they have no control over their actions. Assessment fails to motivate students to learn either intrinsically or extrinsically; students do not feel like learning through assessment.

REFLECTIVE BREAK

Reflect on your own assessment practices to motivate students to learn.

- What assessment practices may lead to intrinsic motivation, self-determined extrinsic motivation, non–self-determined extrinsic motivation, and amotivation?

Involving Students in Assessment
to Increase Motivation

An effective way that teachers can motivate their students is by involving them in the process of assessment through various procedures. For example, teachers can involve students in setting learning goals or achievement goals. The main responsibility for creating these achievement goals rests with the teacher, usually guided by the curriculum and standards. Communicating these goals to students is one effective, practical way of enhancing achievement. Students can collaborate with the teacher to develop additional self-directed outcomes of learning. "If students play even a small role in setting the (learning achievement) target . . . we can gain considerable motivational and therefore achievement benefits" (Stiggins, 2005, p. 244). Stiggins (2005) suggests students keep learning logs as a way to engage them in assessment, increase motivation, and help them reflect on and see their own improvement. Receiving frequent feedback from the teacher can also raise students' awareness of progress.

When students and teachers engage in conversation about assessment, students are encouraged to consider their own cognition, which aids in the learning process. Motivation will continue if students witness and reflect on their growth toward learning goals. Research shows that when students understand and apply self-assessment skills, their achievement increases (Black & Wiliam, 1998b) and that self-assessment plays a significant role in increasing students' motivation to learn. Through self-assessment, students directly observe their own improvement and therefore are more motivated to achieve. By involving students in the assessment processes, teachers encourage students to create a sense of internal responsibility for their achievement. Stiggins (2005) remarks that students "must take responsibility for developing their own sense of control over their success" (p. 296). This, in turn, leads to greater motivation and greater academic success.

REFLECTIVE BREAK

Check that you have used the following six principles to enhance the relationship between motivation and assessment in your own assessment practices. Have you

- shared the learning goals with your students?

- helped your students understand the standards they are working toward?

- involved your students in assessment?

- provided helpful feedback to your students?

- created a positive learning atmosphere in the classroom?

- integrated teaching, learning, and assessment?

Trends and Conclusion

If educators are to "first do no harm" (Taylor & Nolen, 2008, p. 10), they need to continue to focus on the relationship between motivation and assessment and rethink some of the assumptions that they place on testing and assessment. The academic race to be the smartest, most skilled student in the class does not place the focus of learning on improvement or the act of learning itself, but rather on achievement and outcome alone. For assessment to be effective and to enhance, not harm, students' learning, students must compete with themselves to continue to improve, and teachers should use assessment events to help students develop effective learning strategies that will serve them beyond the classroom.

All of the following points ensure high-quality classroom assessment practices that support and enhance student learning—the ultimate goal of instruction:

- Assessment takes place during instruction.

- Knowledge and skills should not be assessed in isolation.

- Students are involved in all aspects of assessment events (assessment *for* learning).

- Assessment is formative.
- Teachers use a combination of assessment *for* learning and assessment *of* learning.

Teachers' classroom assessment plays a central role in and inevitably influences teaching and learning (Cheng, 2008). Stiggins (2005) suggested that, despite its significance, over the last decade classroom assessment became a "victim of gross neglect" (p. 10), receiving little attention in terms of its nature, conduct, and use. In an attempt to spark research designed to improve classroom assessment, a special issue of *Educational Measurement: Issues and Practices* on "Changing the Way Measurement Theorists Think About Classroom Assessment" was published in 2003. Four distinguished measurement specialists called for more research into classroom assessment. They pointed out the need for a new psychometric theory to guide and inform classroom assessment practices and contended that classroom assessment deserves and needs its own theoretical and applied set of procedures. This book is an attempt to address the agenda emphasized in this special issue with the aim to support language classroom teachers with quality classroom assessment knowledge and skills.

References

Alderson, J. C., & Wall, D. (1993). Does washback exist? *Applied Linguistics,* *14,* 115–129.

Bachman, L. F. (1990). *Fundamental considerations in language testing.* Oxford, England: Oxford University Press.

Bachman, L. F. (2000). Modern language testing at the turn of the century: Assuring that what we count counts. *Language Testing, 17*(1), 1–42.

Bachman, L. F., & Palmer, A. S. (1996). *Language testing in practice.* Oxford, England: Oxford University Press.

Black, P., & Wiliam, D. (1998a). Assessment and classroom learning. *Assessment in Education: Principles, Policy and Practice, 5*(1), 7–74.

Black, P., & Wiliam, D. (1998b). Inside the black box: Raising standards through classroom assessment. *Phi Delta Kappan, 80*(2), 139–148.

Breen, M. P., Barratt-Pugh, C., Derewianka, B., House, H., Hudson, C., Lumley, T., & Rohl, M. (1997). *Profiling ESL children: How teachers interpret and use national and state assessment frameworks* (Vols. 1–3). Canberra, Australia: Canberra Department of Employment, Education, Training and Youth Affairs.

Brindley, G. (2007). Editorial. *Language Assessment Quarterly, 4*(1), 1–5.

Brookhart, S. M. (2004). Developing measurement theory for classroom assessment purposes and uses. *Educational Measurement: Issues and Practice, 22*(4), 5–12.

Canale, M., & Swain, M. (1980). Theoretical bases of communicative approach to second language teaching and testing. *Applied Linguistics, 1*(1), 1–47.

Cheng, L. (2005). *Changing language teaching through language testing: A washback study. Studies in Language Testing*. Cambridge, England: Cambridge University Press.

Cheng, L. (2008). Washback, impact and consequences. In E. Shohamy and N. H. Hornberger (Eds.), *Encyclopedia of language and education: Language testing and assessment* (Vol. 7, 2nd ed., pp. 1–13). Chester, England: Springer Science Business Media.

Cheng, L., & DeLuca, C. (2011). Voices from test-takers: Further evidence for test validation and test use. *Educational Assessment, 16*(2), 104–122.

Cheng, L., & Watanabe, Y., with Curtis, A. (Eds.). (2004). *Washback in language testing: Research contexts and methods*. Mahwah, NJ: Lawrence Erlbaum Associates.

Cheng, L., Rogers, T., & Hu, H. (2004). ESL/EFL instructors' classroom assessment practices: Purposes, methods and procedures. *Language Testing, 21*(3), 360–389.

Cheng, L., Rogers, T., & Wang, X. (2008). Assessment purposes and procedures in ESL/EFL classrooms. *Assessment & Evaluation in Higher Education, 33*(1), 9–32.

Cumming, A. (2001). ESL/EFL instructors' practices for writing assessment: Specific purposes or general purposes? *Language Testing, 18*(2), 207–224.

Davison, C. (2007). Views from the chalkface: School-based assessment in Hong Kong. *Language Assessment Quarterly, 4*(1), 37–68.

Dörnyei, Z. (2001). New themes and approaches in second language motivation research. *Annual Review of Applied Linguistics, 21*, 43–59.

Fisher, D., & Frey, N. (2009). Feed up, back, forward. *Educational Leadership, 67*(3), 20–25.

McNamara, T. (2007). Language testing: A question of context. In J. Fox, M. Wesche, D. Bayliss, L. Cheng, C. Turner, & C. Doe (Eds.), *Language testing reconsidered* (pp. 133–140). Ottawa, Canada: University of Ottawa.

Messick, S. (1989). Validity. In R. L. Linn (Ed.), *Educational measurement* (3rd ed., pp. 13–103). New York, NY: Macmillan.

Oller, J. W. (1979). *Language tests at school: A pragmatic approach*. London, England: Longman.

Rea-Dickins, P. (2004). Understanding teachers as agents of assessment. *Language Testing, 21*(3), 249–258.

Ryan, R. M., & Deci, E. L. (2000). Self-determination theory and the facilitation of intrinsic motivation, social development, and well-being. *American Psychologist, 55*, 68–78.

Stiggins, R. J. (2005). *Student-involved assessment for learning* (5th ed.). Upper Saddle River, NJ: Merrill/Prentice Hall.

Sun, Y., & Cheng, L. (2013). Teachers' grading practices: Meanings and values assigned. *Assessment in Education.* doi:10.1080/0969594X .2013.768207

Taylor, C. S., & Nolen, S. B. (2008). *Classroom assessment: Supporting teaching and learning in real classrooms* (2nd ed.). Mahwah, NJ: Pearson Education.

Tully, M. G. (2004). *Instructor's manual and test bank for McMilan* (3rd ed.). Boston, MA: Pearson.

Also Available in the English Language Teacher Development Series

Reflective Teaching (Thomas S. C. Farrell)

Teaching Listening (Ekaterina Nemtchinova)

Teaching Pronunciation (John Murphy)

Language Classroom Assessment (Liying Cheng)

Cooperative Learning and Teaching (George Jacobs & Harumi Kimura)

Classroom Research for Language Teachers (Tim Stewart)

Teaching Digital Literacies (Joel Bloch)

Teaching Reading (Richard Day)

Teaching Grammar (William Crawford)

Teaching Vocabulary (Michael Lessard-Clouston)

Teaching Writing (Zuzana Tomas, Ilka Kostka, & Jennifer A. Mott-Smith)

English Language Teachers as Administrators (Dan Tannacito)

Content-Based Instruction (Margo Dellicarpini & Orlando Alonso)

Teaching English as an International Language
(Ali Fuad Selvi & Bedrettin Yazan)

Teaching Speaking (Tasha Bleistein, Melissa K. Smith, & Marilyn Lewis)

www.tesol.org/bookstore
tesolpubs@brightkey.net
Request a copy for review
Request a Distributor Policy